THE SCHOOL FOR WIVES

ALSO BY RICHARD WILBUR

The Beautiful Changes and Other Poems

Ceremony and Other Poems

A Bestiary
(editor, with Alexander Calder)

Molière's *The Misanthrope*
(translator)

Things of This World
(poems)

Poems 1943–1956

Candide
(comic opera, with Lillian Hellman)

Poe: Complete Poems
(editor)

Advice to a Prophet and Other Poems

Molière's *Tartuffe*
(translator)

The Poems of Richard Wilbur

Loudmouse
(for children)

Shakespeare: Poems
(co-editor, with Alfred Harbage)

Walking to Sleep: New Poems and Translations

JEAN BAPTISTE POQUELIN DE MOLIÈRE

The School for Wives

COMEDY IN FIVE ACTS, 1662

TRANSLATED INTO ENGLISH VERSE BY
RICHARD WILBUR

A HARVEST BOOK
HARCOURT BRACE JOVANOVICH, INC.
NEW YORK

Drawings by Enrico Arno

ISBN 0-15-679501-9
Library of Congress Catalog Card Number: 70–153693
Printed in the United States of America
A B C D E F G H I J

Certain scenes of this translation have appeared in the *New York Quarterly* and in *Countermeasures*.

To the memory of
Louis Jouvet
1887–1951

INTRODUCTION

As Dorante says in the *Critique de l'École des femmes,* a comic monster need not lack all attractive qualities. Arnolphe, the hero of Molière's first great verse comedy, is a forty-two-year-old provincial bourgeois whom it is possible to like, up to a point, for his coarse heartiness and his generosity with money. He is, however, a madman, and his alienation is of a harmful and unlovable kind. What ails him is a deep general insecurity, which has somehow been focused into a specific terror of being cuckolded. In fear of that humiliation, he has put off marriage until what, for the seventeenth century, was a very ripe age; meanwhile, he has buttressed his frail vanity by gloating over such of his neighbors as have been deceived by their wives. He has, furthermore, become the guardian of a four-year-old child, Agnès, with a view to shaping her into his idea of a perfect bride, and for thirteen years has had her trained to be docile and ignorant. It is his theory, based upon much anxious observation, that a stupid wife will not shame her husband by infidelity. As the play begins, Arnolphe is about to marry Agnès and achieve a double satisfaction: he will quiet his long trepidation by marrying safely, and he will have the prideful pleasure of showing the world how to rig an infallible alliance. It goes without saying that poor, stultified Agnès is not his object but his victim.

Arnolphe, then, is one of Molière's coercers of life. Like Tartuffe, he proposes to manipulate the world for his own ends, and the play is one long joke about the futility of selfish calculation. Agnès is guileless; her young man, Horace, is a rash bumbler who informs his rival of all that he does and means to do; yet despite Arnolphe's mature canniness, and his twenty years' pondering and plotting, he loses out to a *jeune innocente* and a *jeune écervelé.* Why? There is much high talk in the play, especially from Arnolphe, of cruel destiny, fate, and the stars, and this contributes, as J. D. Hubert has noted, to an effect of "burlesque tragedy"; it is not implacable fate, however, but ridiculous chance which repeatedly spoils Arnolphe's designs. And indeed, the plans of other characters, even when benign, meet constantly with the fortuitous: if Horace achieves his goal, it is certainly not because his blundering intrigues have mastered circumstance; and though Oronte and Enrique accomplish the premeditated union of their children, *le hasard* has already brought the pair together. The play seems to assert that any effort to impose expectations on life will meet with surprises, and that a narrow, rigid, and inhumane demand will not be honored by Nature.

The plot of *L'École des femmes* has often been criticized for its unlikelihood. Doubtless Molière was careless of the fact, since, as W. G. Moore has written, "The plot is not the main thing at all. . . . The high points of the play are not the turning points of the action; they are moments when the clash of youth and age, of spontaneity and automatism, takes shape in speech and scene." And yet it may not be too much to say that the absurdity of the plot is expressive, that it presents us with the world as Arnolphe is bound to experience it. To an obsessed man, the world will be full of exasperating irrelevancies: in this case, a dead kitten, a ribbon, the inopportune chatter of a notary. Similarly, a man who has for years left nothing to chance in the prosecution of a maniacal plan, and who encounters difficulties on the very eve of success, will experience the world as a chaos of disruptive accidents, a storm of casualty: in this case, an old friend's son will by chance gain the affections of Arnolphe's intended; in repeated chance meetings he will subject Arnolphe, whose new title he chances not to know, to tormenting confidences; Oronte and Enrique will chance to arrive in town on what was to have been Arnolphe's wedding day, and will reveal the true identity of the young woman whom Arnolphe once chanced to adopt. It is all too much, for Arnolphe and for us, and in the last-minute breathless summary of Enrique's story, delivered by Chrysalde and Oronte in alternating couplets, Molière both burlesques a species of comic dénouement and acknowledges the outrageousness of his own. At the same time, for this reader, the gay arbitrariness of the close celebrates a truth which is central to the comic vision—that life will not be controlled, but makes a fluent resistance to all crabbèd constraint. The most triumphant demonstration of life's (or Nature's) irrepressibility occurs within Arnolphe himself, when, after so many years of coldly exploiting Agnès for his pride's sake, he becomes vulnerably human by falling in love with her.

Spontaneity versus automatism, life's happy refusal to conform to cranky plans and theories: such terms describe the play for me. Some, however, may wish to be less general, and to discern here a thesis play about, say, education. This comedy is, indeed, permeated with the themes of instruction and learning. Arnolphe has Agnès minimally educated, so that she will have no attractive accomplishments; the nuns teach her to pray, spin, and sew (and somehow, though it is against her guardian's orders, she also learns to read). In Act III, Arnolphe himself becomes her teacher, or, rather, her priest, and with repeated threats of hell-fire informs her that the function of a wife is to live wholly for her husband, in absolute subjection. *The Maxims of Marriage*, which Agnès is then given to study, are likened by Arnolphe to the rules which a novice must learn on entering a convent; and very like they are, counseling as they do a cloistered and sacrificial life devoted to the worship of one's husband. Arnolphe's whole teaching is that the purpose of marriage is to preserve the husband's honor, which is like saying that the purpose of dancing is not to break a leg; and his whole education of Agnès is intended to incapacitate her for adultery by rendering her spiritless and uninteresting. There are moments, I think, when other characters burlesque Arnolphe as educator: the manservant Alain, informing Georgette in Act II, Scene 2 that "womankind is . . . the soup of man," caricatures his master's attitude toward women, as well as his patronizing pedagogical style; and the notary, torrentially instructing Arnolphe in contract law, resembles in his pedantic formulae the Arnolphe of the smug thesis, the airtight plan, and the *Maxims*. Much else in the play might be seen as extending the motif of instruction: Arnolphe rehearsing or drilling his servants; Chrysalde lecturing Arnolphe on the temperate view of cuckoldry; Arnolphe schooling himself in the causes of marital disaster, being guided by a Greek who counseled Augustus, or advising Oronte on the use of paternal power. But what is more surely pertinent, and stands in opposition to Arnolphe's kind of schooling, is the transformation of Horace and Agnès by that *grand maître*, Love. When we first meet him, Horace is a pretty-boy very full of himself and quite capable of seducing Agnès, but by the fifth act he has come to esteem and cherish her, and had "rather die than do her any wrong." Agnès, awakened by love to her own childish ignorance and dependence, proceeds like Juliet to develop gumption and resourcefulness, and discovers a wit which is the more devastating because of her continuing simplicity.

The play is full of "education"; granted. But it cannot convincingly be interpreted as a thesis play *about* education. What can Molière be said to advocate? Latin for women? The inclusion of love in the curriculum? Clearly Molière had a low opinion of Agnès' convent schooling, which was rather standard for the age; what really interests him, however, is not the deficiencies of such schooling but Arnolphe's ill-intended use of them. Similarly, Molière is concerned not with religion but with Arnolphe's selfish and Orgon-like abuse of it, his turning it into a bludgeon. Nor does he comment on parental authority in itself, but, rather, on Arnolphe's attempt to exploit it for his own ends. It will not do, in short, for the contemporary reader or director to inject this play with Student Unrest or Women's Liberation,

[*Introduction*]

or to descry in it a Generation Gap. That way lies melo-
drama.

Any director of this English version will have to solve
for himself certain problems of interpretation and staging,
but I shall say what I think. It is my own decided opinion
that Chrysalde is *not* a cuckold, and that Arnolphe's second
speech in Act I, Scene 1 is a bit of crude and objectionable
ribbing. Chrysalde's discourses about cuckoldry should be
regarded, I think, both as frequently dubious "reasoning" and
as bear-baiting; a good actor would know where to modulate
between them. Arnolphe's distaste for fuss and sophistication
is likely to impress some as an endearing quality, but I do
not see it so; rather, it is of a piece with the man's anxiety
to prove himself superior to a society whose ridicule he
fears, and like the "honesty" of the *Misanthrope*'s Alceste, it
entails posturing and bad faith. Finally, there is the fact that
much of the slapstick in the plot—the throwing of the brick,
Horace's tumble from the ladder—occurs off stage, and that
the on-stage proceedings consist in fair part of long speeches.
I should be sorry to see any director right this apparent im-
balance by introducing too much pie-throwing and bottom-
pinching of his own invention. Once again, Dorante gives
Molière's point of view: the long speeches, he says, "are themselves actions," involving incessant ironic *interplay* between
speakers and hearers. To take the most obvious example,
Horace's addresses to Arnolphe are rendered wonderfully
"busy" by the fact that he does not know he is addressing
M. de la Souche, that Arnolphe cannot enlighten him, and
that Arnolphe must continually struggle to conceal his glee or
anguish. To add any great amount of farcical "business" to
such complex comedy would be to divert in an unfortunate
sense.

This translation has aimed at a thought-for-thought fidelity,
and has sought in its verse to avoid the metronomic, which
is particularly fatal on the stage: I have sometimes been very

[*Introduction*]

limber indeed, as in the line "He's the most hideous Christian I ever did see." For a few words or phrases I am indebted to earlier English versions in blank verse or prose. I must also thank Jan Miel for helping me to improve these remarks; Robert Hollander, Stephen Porter, and William Jay Smith for reading and criticizing the translation; and John Berryman for encouraging me to undertake it.

R. W.

Wesleyan University
November, 1970

THE SCHOOL FOR WIVES

CHARACTERS

ARNOLPHE, also known as MONSIEUR DE LA SOUCHE

AGNÈS, an innocent young girl, Arnolphe's ward

HORACE, Agnès' lover, Oronte's son

ALAIN, a peasant, Arnolphe's manservant

GEORGETTE, a peasant woman, servant to Arnolphe

CHRYSALDE, a friend of Arnolphe's

ENRIQUE, Chrysalde's brother-in-law, Agnès' father

ORONTE, Horace's father and Arnolphe's old friend

A NOTARY

The scene is a square in a provincial city.

First produced by the Phoenix Theatre, *New York, on February 16, 1971*

Act 1

SCENE ONE

CHRYSALDE

So, you're resolved to give this girl your hand?

ARNOLPHE

Tomorrow I shall marry her, as planned.

CHRYSALDE

We're quite alone here, and we can discuss
Your case with no one overhearing us:
Shall I speak openly, and as your friend?
This plan—for your sake—troubles me no end.
I must say that, from every point of view,
Taking a wife is a rash step for you.

ARNOLPHE

You think so? Might it be, friend, that you base
Your fears for me upon your own sad case?
Cuckolds would have us think that all who marry
Acquire a set of horns as corollary.

CHRYSALDE

Fate gives men horns, and fate can't be withstood;
To fret about such matters does no good.
What makes me fear for you is the way you sneer
At every luckless husband of whom you hear.
You know that no poor cuckold, great or small,
Escapes your wit; you mock them one and all,
And take delight in making boisterous mention
Of all intrigues which come to your attention.

ARNOLPHE

Why not? What other town on earth is known
For husbands so long-suffering as our own?
Can we not all too readily bring to mind
Ill-treated dupes of every shape and kind?
One husband's rich; his helpmeet shares the wealth
With paramours who cuckold him by stealth;
Another, with a scarcely kinder fate,
Sees other men heap gifts upon his mate—
Who frees his mind of jealous insecurity
By saying that they're tributes to her purity.
One cuckold impotently storms and rants;
Another mildly bows to circumstance,
And when some gallant calls to see his spouse,
Discreetly takes his hat and leaves the house.
One wife, confiding in her husband, mentions
A swain who bores her with his warm attentions;
The husband smugly pities the poor swain
For all his efforts—which are *not* in vain.
Another wife explains her wealthy state
By saying that she's held good cards of late;
Her husband thanks the Lord and gives Him praise,

Not guessing what bad game she truly plays.
Thus, all about us, there are themes for wit;
May I not, as an observer, jest a bit?
May I not laugh at—

CHRYSALDE

        Yes; but remember, do,
That those you mock may someday mock at you.
Now, I hear gossip, I hear what people say
About the latest scandals of the day,
But whatsoever I'm told, I never hear it
With wicked glee and in a gloating spirit.
I keep my counsel; and though I may condemn
Loose wives, and husbands who put up with them,
And though I don't propose, you may be sure,
To endure the wrongs which some weak men endure,
Still, I am never heard to carp and crow,
For tables have been known to turn, you know,
And there's no man who can predict, in fact,
How in such circumstances he would act.
In consequence, should fate bestow on me
What all must fear, the horns of cuckoldry,
The world would treat me gently, I believe,
And be content with laughing up its sleeve.
There are, in fact, some kindly souls who might
Commiserate me in my sorry plight.
But you, dear fellow, with you it's not the same.
I say once more, you play a dangerous game.
Since with your jeering tongue you plague the lives
Of men who are unlucky in their wives,
And persecute them like a fiend from Hell,
Take care lest someday you be jeered as well.
If the least whisper about your wife were heard,

9

They'd mock you from the housetops, mark my word.
What's more—

ARNOLPHE

      Don't worry, friend; I'm not a fool.
I shan't expose myself to ridicule.
I know the tricks and ruses, shrewd and sly,
Which wives employ, and cheat their husbands by;
I know that women can be deep and clever;
But I've arranged to be secure forever:
So simple is the girl I'm going to wed
That I've no fear of horns upon my head.

CHRYSALDE

Simple! You mean to bind yourself for life—

ARNOLPHE

A man's not simple to take a simple wife.
Your wife, no doubt, is a wise, virtuous woman,
But brightness, as a rule, is a bad omen,
And I know men who've undergone much pain
Because they married girls with too much brain.
I want no intellectual, if you please,
Who'll talk of nothing but her Tuesday teas,
Who'll frame lush sentiments in prose and verse
And fill the house with wits, and fops, and worse,
While I, as her dull husband, stand about
Like a poor saint whose candles have gone out.
No, keep your smart ones; I've no taste for such.
Women who versify know far too much.
I want a wife whose thought is not sublime,

Who has no notion what it is to rhyme,
And who, indeed, if she were asked in some
Insipid parlor game, "What rhymes with drum?"
Would answer in all innocence, "A fife."
In short, I want an unaccomplished wife,
And there are four things only she must know:
To say her prayers, love me, spin, and sew.

CHRYSALDE

Stupidity's your cup of tea, I gather.

ARNOLPHE

I'd choose an ugly, stupid woman rather
Than a great beauty who was over-wise.

CHRYSALDE

But wit and beauty—

ARNOLPHE

Virtue is what I prize.

CHRYSALDE

But how can you expect an idiot
To know what's virtuous and what is not?
Not only would it be a lifelong bore
To have a senseless wife, but what is more,
I hardly think you could depend upon her
To guard her husband's forehead from dishonor.
If a bright woman breaks her wedding vow,

She knows what she is doing, anyhow;
A simpleton, however, can commit
Adultery without suspecting it.

ARNOLPHE

To that fine argument I can but say
What Pantagruel says in Rabelais:
Preach and harangue from now till Whitsuntide
Against my preference for a stupid bride;
You'll be amazed to find, when you have ceased,
That I've not been persuaded in the least.

CHRYSALDE

So be it.

ARNOLPHE

                Each man has his own design
For wedded bliss, and I shall follow mine.
I'm rich, and so can take a wife who'll be
Dependent, in the least respect, on me—
A sweet, submissive girl who cannot claim
To have brought me riches or an ancient name.
The gentle, meek expression which she wore
Endeared Agnès to me when she was four;
Her mother being poor, I felt an urge
To make the little thing my ward and charge,
And the good peasant woman was most pleased
To grant my wish, and have her burden eased.
In a small convent, far from the haunts of man,
The girl was reared according to my plan:
I told the nuns what means must be employed
To keep her growing mind a perfect void,

And, God be praised, they had entire success.
As a grown girl, her simple-mindedness
Is such that I thank Heaven for granting me
A bride who suits my wishes to a T.
She's out of the convent now, and since my gate
Stands open to society, early and late,
I keep her here, in another house I own,
Where no one calls, and she can be alone:
And, to protect her artless purity,
I've hired two servants as naïve as she.
I've told you all this so that you'll understand
With what great care my marriage has been planned;
And now, to clinch my story, I invite
You, my dear friend, to dine with her tonight;
I want you to examine her, and decide
Whether or not my choice is justified.

CHRYSALDE

Delighted.

ARNOLPHE

You'll gain, I think, a lively sense
Of her sweet person and her innocence.

CHRYSALDE

As to her innocence, what you've related
Leaves little doubt—

ARNOLPHE

My friend, 't was understated.
Her utter naïveté keeps me in stitches.

I laugh so that I almost burst my breeches.
You won't believe this, but the other day
She came and asked me in a puzzled way,
And with a manner touchingly sincere,
If children are begotten through the ear.

CHRYSALDE

I'm happy indeed, Monsieur Arnolphe—

ARNOLPHE

For shame!
Why must you always use my former name?

CHRYSALDE

I'm used to it, I suppose. What's more, I find
That *de la Souche* forever slips my mind.
What in the devil has persuaded you
To debaptize yourself at forty-two
And take a lordly title which you base
On an old tree stump at your country place?

ARNOLPHE

The name La Souche goes with the property
And sounds much better than Arnolphe to me.

CHRYSALDE

But why forsake the name your fathers bore
For one that's fantasy and nothing more?
Yet lately that's become the thing to do.

[*Act One · Scene One*]

I am reminded—no offense to you—
Of a peasant named Gros-Pierre, who owned a small
Parcel of land, an acre or so in all;
He dug a muddy ditch around the same
And took Monsieur de l'Isle for his new name.

ARNOLPHE

I can dispense with stories of that kind.
My name is de la Souche, if you don't mind.
I like that title, and it's mine by right;
To address me otherwise is impolite.

CHRYSALDE

Your new name is employed by few, at best;
Much of your mail, I've noticed, comes addressed—

ARNOLPHE

I don't mind that, from such as haven't been told;
But you—

CHRYSALDE

Enough. Enough. No need to scold.
I hereby promise that, at our next meeting,
"Good day, Monsieur de la Souche" shall be my greeting.

ARNOLPHE

Farewell. I'm going to knock now on my door
And let them know that I'm in town once more.

[*Act One · Scene One*]

CHRYSALDE, *aside, as he moves off*

The man's quite mad. A lunatic, in fact.

ARNOLPHE, *alone*

On certain subjects he's a trifle cracked.
It's curious to see with what devotion
A man will cling to some quite pointless notion.
Ho, there!

SCENE TWO

ALAIN, GEORGETTE, ARNOLPHE

ALAIN, *within*

Who's knocking?

ARNOLPHE

      Ho! (*Aside:*) They'll greet me, after
My ten days' trip, with smiles and happy laughter.

ALAIN

Who's there?

ARNOLPHE

It's I.

ALAIN

Georgette!

GEORGETTE

What?

[*Act One · Scene Two*]

ALAIN

Open below!

GEORGETTE

Do it yourself!

ALAIN

You do it!

GEORGETTE

I won't go!

ALAIN

I won't go either!

ARNOLPHE

Gracious servants, these,
To leave me standing here. Ho! If you please!

GEORGETTE

Who's there?

ARNOLPHE

Your master.

[*Act One · Scene Two*]

GEORGETTE

Alain!

ALAIN

What?

GEORGETTE

Go lift the latch!

It's him.

ALAIN

You do it.

GEORGETTE

I'm getting the fire to catch.

ALAIN

I'm keeping the cat from eating the canary.

ARNOLPHE

Whoever doesn't admit me, and in a hurry,
Will get no food for four long days, and more.
Aha!

GEORGETTE

I'll get it; what are you coming for?

[*Act One · Scene Two*]

ALAIN

Why you, not me? That's a sneaky trick to play!

GEORGETTE

Get out of the way.

ALAIN

No, *you* get out of the way.

GEORGETTE

I want to open that door.

ALAIN

I want to, too.

GEORGETTE

You won't.

ALAIN

And you won't either.

GEORGETTE

Neither will you.

ARNOLPHE, *to himself*

My patience with these two amazes me.

20

[*Act One · Scene Two*]

ALAIN

I've opened the door, Sir.

GEORGETTE

No, I did it! See?
'T was I.

ALAIN

If only the master, here, weren't present,
I'd—

ARNOLPHE, *receiving a blow from Alain,*
meant for Georgette

Blast you!

ALAIN

Sorry, Sir.

ARNOLPHE

You clumsy peasant!

ALAIN

It's her fault too, Sir.

ARNOLPHE

Both of you, stop this row.
I want to question you; no nonsense, now.
Alain, is everything going smoothly here?

[*Act One · Scene Two*]

ALAIN

Well, Sir, we're—
    (*Arnolphe removes Alain's hat; Alain
    obliviously puts it back on.*)
        Well, Sir—
          (*Hat business again.*)
            Well, thank God, Sir, we're—
        (*Arnolphe removes Alain's hat a third time,
        and throws it to the ground.*)

ARNOLPHE

Where did you learn, you lout, to wear a hat
While talking to your master? Answer me that.

ALAIN

You're right, I'm wrong.

ARNOLPHE

          Now, have Agnès come down.
    (*To Georgette:*)
Was she unhappy while I was out of town?

GEORGETTE

Unhappy? No.

ARNOLPHE

    No?

22

GEORGETTE

Yes.

ARNOLPHE

For what reason, then?

GEORGETTE

Well, she kept thinking you'd be back again,
So that whatever passed on the avenue—
Horse, mule, or ass—she thought it must be you.

SCENE THREE

AGNÈS, ALAIN, GEORGETTE, ARNOLPHE

ARNOLPHE

Her needlework in hand! That's a good sign.
Well, well, Agnès, I'm back and feeling fine.
Are you glad to see me?

AGNÈS

                              Oh, yes, Sir; thank the Lord.

ARNOLPHE

I'm glad to see you too, my little ward.
I take it everything has been all right?

AGNÈS

Except for the fleas, which bothered me last night.

ARNOLPHE

Well, there'll be someone soon to drive them away.

AGNÈS

I shall be glad of that.

24

[*Act One · Scene Three*]

ARNOLPHE

        Yes, I dare say.
What are you making?

AGNÈS

        A headpiece, Sir, for me;
Your nightshirts are all finished, as you'll see.

ARNOLPHE

Excellent. Well, upstairs with you, my dear:
I'll soon come back and see you, never fear;
There's serious talk in which we must engage.
    (*Exeunt all but Arnolphe.*)
O learned ladies, heroines of the age,
Gushers of sentiment, I say that you,
For all your verse, and prose, and billets-doux,
Your novels, and your bright accomplishments,
Can't match this good and modest ignorance.

SCENE FOUR

ARNOLPHE

What does her lack of money matter to me?
What matters— Oh! What's this? No! Can it be?
I'm dreaming. Yes, it's he, my dear friend's boy.
Well!

HORACE

Sir!

ARNOLPHE

Horace!

HORACE

Arnolphe!

ARNOLPHE

Ah, what a joy!
How long have you been in town?

26

HORACE

Nine days.

ARNOLPHE

Ah, so.

HORACE

I called at your house, in vain, a week ago.

ARNOLPHE

I'd left for the country.

HORACE

Yes, you were three days gone.

ARNOLPHE

How quickly children grow! How time rolls on!
I am amazed that you're so big and tall.
I can remember when you were—
　　　　(*He makes a gesture of measuring from the floor.*)
　　　　　　　　　　that small.

HORACE

Yes, time goes by.

ARNOLPHE

But come now, tell me of
Oronte, your father, whom I esteem and love:

27

How's my old friend? Still spry and full of zest?
In all that's his, I take an interest.
Alas, it's four years since I talked with him,
And we've not written in the interim.

HORACE

Seigneur Arnolphe, he's spry enough for two;
He gave me this little note to give to you,
But now he writes me that he's coming here
Himself, for reasons not entirely clear.
Some fellow-townsman of yours, whom you may know,
Went to America fourteen years ago;
He's come back rich. Do you know of whom I speak?

ARNOLPHE

No. Did the letter give his name?

HORACE

Enrique.

ARNOLPHE

No . . . no . . .

HORACE

My father writes as if I ought
To recognize that name, but I do not.
He adds that he and Enrique will soon set out
On some great errand that he's vague about.

28

[*Act One · Scene Four*]

ARNOLPHE

I long to see your father, that sterling man.
I'll welcome him as royally as I can.
    (*He reads the note from Oronte.*)
A friendly letter needn't flatter and fuss.
All this politeness is superfluous,
And even without his asking, I'd have desired
To lend you any money you required.

HORACE

I'll take you at your word, Sir. Can you advance
Fifty *pistoles* or so, by any chance?

ARNOLPHE

I'm grateful that you let me be of use,
And what you ask, I happily can produce.
Just keep the purse.

HORACE

Here—

ARNOLPHE

        Forget the I.O.U.
Now, how does our town impress you? Tell me, do.

HORACE

It's rich in people, sublime in architecture,
And full of fine amusements, I conjecture.

[*Act One · Scene Four*]

ARNOLPHE

There's pleasure here for every taste; and those
The world calls gallants, ladies' men, or beaux
Find here the sport on which their hearts are set,
Since every woman in town's a born coquette.
Our ladies, dark or fair, are pliant creatures;
Their husbands, likewise, have permissive natures;
Oh, it's a capital game; it's often made
Me double up with mirth to see it played.
But you've already broken some hearts, I'd guess;
Have you no gallant conquest to confess?
Cuckolds are made by such as you, young man,
And looks like yours buy more than money can.

HORACE

Well, since you ask, I'll lay my secrets bare.
I *have* been having a covert love affair—
Which, out of friendship, I shall now unveil.

ARNOLPHE

Good, good; 't will be another rakish tale
Which I can put into my repertory.

HORACE

Sir, I must beg you: don't divulge my story.

ARNOLPHE

Of course not.

HORACE

As you know, Sir, in these matters,
One word let slip can leave one's hopes in tatters.
To put the business plainly, then, my heart's
Been lost to a lady dwelling in these parts.
My overtures, I'm very pleased to state,
Have found her ready to reciprocate,
And not to boast, or slur her reputation,
I think I'm in a hopeful situation.

ARNOLPHE, *laughing*

Who is she?

HORACE

A girl whose beauty is past telling,
And yonder red-walled mansion is her dwelling.
She's utterly naïve, because a blind
Fool has sequestered her from humankind,
And yet, despite the ignorance in which
He keeps her, she has charms that can bewitch;
She's most engaging, and conveys a sense
Of sweetness against which there's no defense.
But you, perhaps, have seen this star of love
Whose many graces I'm enamoured of.
Her name's Agnès.

ARNOLPHE, *aside*

Oh, death!

HORACE

> The man, I hear,
> Is called La Zousse, La Source, or something queer;
> I didn't pay much attention to the name.
> He's rich, I gather, but his wits are lame,
> And he's accounted a ridiculous fellow.
> D'you know him?

ARNOLPHE, *aside*

> Ugh, what a bitter pill to swallow!

HORACE

I said, do you know him?

ARNOLPHE

> Yes, I do, in a way.

HORACE

He's a dolt, isn't he?

ARNOLPHE

> Oh!

HORACE

> What? What did you say?
> He is, I take it. And a jealous idiot, too?
> An ass? I see that all they said was true.

32

Well, to repeat, I love Agnès, a girl
Who is, to say the least, an orient pearl,
And it would be a sin for such a treasure
To be subjected to that old fool's pleasure.
Henceforth, my thoughts and efforts shall combine
To break his jealous hold and make her mine;
This purse, which I made bold to borrow, will lend
Me great assistance toward that worthy end.
As you well know, whatever means one tries,
Money's the key to every enterprise,
And this sweet metal, which all men hanker for,
Promotes our conquests, whether in love or war.
You look disturbed, Sir; can it be that you
Do not approve of what I mean to do?

ARNOLPHE

No; I was thinking—

HORACE

    I'm boring you. Farewell, then.
I'll soon drop by, to express my thanks again.

ARNOLPHE, *to himself*

How could this happen—

HORACE, *returning*

    Again, Sir, I entreat
You not to tell my secret; be discreet.
   (*He leaves.*)

33

[*Act One · Scene Four*]

ARNOLPHE, *to himself*

I'm thunderstruck.

HORACE, *returning*

Above all, don't inform
My father; he might raise a dreadful storm.
(*He leaves.*)

ARNOLPHE (*He expects Horace to return again;
that not occurring, he talks to himself.*)

Oh! . . . What I've suffered during this conversation!
No soul has ever endured such agitation.
With what imprudence, and how hastily
He came and told the whole affair . . . to me!
He didn't know I'd taken a new title;
Still, what a rash and blundering recital!
I should, however, have kept myself in hand,
So as to learn what strategy he's planned,
And prompt his indiscretion, and discover
To what extent he has become her lover.
Come, I'll catch up with him; he can't be far;
I'll learn from him precisely how things are.
Alas, I'm trembling; I fear some further blow;
One can discover more than one wants to know.

SCENE ONE

ARNOLPHE

ARNOLPHE

It's just as well, no doubt, that I should fail
To catch him—that I somehow lost his trail:
For I could not have managed to dissemble
The turbulence of soul which makes me tremble;
He'd have perceived my present near-despair,
Of which it's best that he be unaware.
But I'm not one to be resigned and meek
And turn this little fop the other cheek.
I'll stop him; and the first thing I must do
Is find out just how far they've gone, those two.
This matter involves my honor, which I prize;
The girl's my wife already, in my eyes;
If she's been tarnished, I am covered with shame,
And all she's done reflects on my good name.
Oh, why did I take that trip? Oh, dear, oh, dear.
          (*He knocks at his door.*)

SCENE TWO

ALAIN

Ah! *This* time, Sir—

ARNOLPHE

        Hush! Both of you come here:
This way, this way. Come, hurry! Do as you're told!

GEORGETTE

You frighten me; you make my blood run cold.

ARNOLPHE

So! In my absence, you have disobeyed me!
The two of you, in concert, have betrayed me!

GEORGETTE, *falling on her knees*

Don't eat me, Sir; don't eat me alive, I beg.

ALAIN, *aside*

I'd swear some mad dog's nipped him in the leg.

38

ARNOLPHE, *aside*

Oof! I'm too tense to speak. I'd like to shed
These blasted clothes. I'm burning up with dread.
        (*To Alain and Georgette:*)
You cursèd scoundrels, while I was gone you let
A man into this house—
        (*To Alain, who has made a move to flee:*)
                No, not just yet!
Tell me at once— (*To Georgette:*) Don't move! I want
  you two
To tell me— Whff! I mean to learn from you—
        (*Alain and Georgette rise and try to escape.*)
If anyone moves, I'll squash him like a louse.
Now tell me, how did that man get into my house?
Well, speak! Come, hurry. Quickly! Time is fleeting!
Let's hèar it! Speak!

ALAIN *and* GEORGETTE, *falling on their knees*

Oh! Oh!

GEORGETTE

My heart's stopped beating.

ALAIN

I'm dying.

ARNOLPHE, *aside*

I'm sweating, and I need some air.
I must calm down: I'll walk around the square.

39

When I saw him in his cradle, I didn't know
What he'd grow up and do to me. O woe!
Perhaps—yes, I'd do better to receive
The truth from her own lips, I now believe.
I'll mute my rage as well as I know how;
Patience, my wounded heart! Beat softly, now!
     (*To Alain and Georgette:*)
Get up, and go inside, and call Agnès.
Wait. (*Aside:*) That way her surprise would be the less.
They'd warn her of my anger, I don't doubt.
I'd best go in myself and bring her out.
     (*To Alain and Georgette:*)
Wait here.

SCENE THREE

GEORGETTE

    God help us, but his rage is terrible!
The way he glared at me—it was unbearable.
He's the most hideous Christian I ever did see.

ALAIN

He's vexed about that man, as I said he'd be.

GEORGETTE

But why does he order us, with barks and roars,
Never to let the mistress go outdoors?
Why does he want us to conceal her here
From all the world, and let no man come near?

ALAIN

It's jealousy that makes him treat her so.

GEORGETTE

But how did he get like that, I'd like to know?

[*Act Two · Scene Three*]

ALAIN

It comes of being jealous, I assume.

GEORGETTE

But why is he jealous? Why must he rage and fume?

ALAIN

Well, jealousy—listen carefully, Georgette—
Is a thing—a thing—which makes a man upset,
And makes him close his doors to everyone.
I'm going to give you a comparison,
So that you'll clearly understand the word.
Suppose you were eating soup, and it occurred
That someone tried to take what you were eating:
Wouldn't you feel like giving him a beating?

GEORGETTE

Yes, I see that.

ALAIN

        Then grasp this, if you can.
Womankind is, in fact, the soup of man,
And when a man perceives that others wish
To dip their dirty fingers into his dish,
His temper flares, and bursts into a flame.

GEORGETTE

Yes. But not everybody feels the same.
Some husbands seem to be delighted when
Their wives consort with fancy gentlemen.

42

ALAIN

Not every husband is the greedy kind
That wants to have it all.

GEORGETTE

                    If I'm not blind,
He's coming back.

ALAIN

            It's he; your eyes are keen.

GEORGETTE

He's scowling.

ALAIN

            That's because he's feeling mean.

SCENE FOUR

ARNOLPHE, ALAIN, GEORGETTE

ARNOLPHE, *aside*

A certain Greek presumed once to advise
The great Augustus, and his words were wise:
When you are vexed, he said, do not forget,
Before you act, to say the alphabet,
So as to cool your temper, and prevent
Rash moves which later on you might repent.
In dealing with Agnès, I have applied
That counsel, and I've bidden her come outside,
Under the pretext of a morning stroll,
So that I can relieve my jangled soul
By seeking dulcetly to draw her out
And learn the truth, and put an end to doubt.
(*Calling:*) Come out, Agnès. (*To Alain and Georgette:*)
   Go in.

SCENE FIVE

ARNOLPHE, AGNÈS

ARNOLPHE

The weather's mild.

AGNÈS

Oh, yes.

ARNOLPHE

Most pleasant.

AGNÈS

Indeed!

ARNOLPHE

What news, my child?

AGNÈS

The kitten died.

ARNOLPHE

Too bad, but what of that?
All men are mortal, my dear, and so's a cat.
While I was gone, no doubt it rained and poured?

AGNÈS

No.

ARNOLPHE

You were bored, perhaps?

AGNÈS

I'm never bored.

ARNOLPHE

During my ten days' absence, what did you do?

AGNÈS

Six nightshirts, I believe; six nightcaps, too.

ARNOLPHE, *after a pause*

My dear Agnès, this world's a curious thing.
What wicked talk one hears, what gossiping!
While I was gone, or so the neighbors claim,
There was a certain strange young man who came
To call upon you here, and was received.
But such a slander's not to be believed,
And I would wager that their so-called news—

AGNÈS

Heavens! Don't wager; you'd be sure to lose.

ARNOLPHE

What! Is it true, then, that a man—

AGNÈS

                               Oh, yes.
In fact, he all but lived at this address.

ARNOLPHE, *aside*

That frank reply would seem to demonstrate
That she's still free of guile, at any rate.
    (*Aloud:*)
But I gave orders, Agnès, as I recall,
That you were to see no one, no one at all.

AGNÈS

I disobeyed you, but when I tell you why,
You'll say that you'd have done the same as I.

ARNOLPHE

Perhaps; well, tell me how this thing occurred.

AGNÈS

It's the most amazing story you ever heard.
I was sewing, out on the balcony, in the breeze,

47

When I noticed someone strolling under the trees.
It was a fine young man, who caught my eye
And made me a deep bow as he went by.
I, not to be convicted of a lack
Of manners, very quickly nodded back.
At once, the young man bowed to me again.
I bowed to him a second time, and then
It wasn't very long until he made
A third deep bow, which I of course repaid.
He left, but kept returning, and as he passed,
He'd bow, each time, more gracefully than the last,
While I, observing as he came and went,
Gave each new bow a fresh acknowledgment.
Indeed, had night not fallen, I declare
I think that I might still be sitting there,
And bowing back each time he bowed to me,
For fear he'd think me less polite than he.

ARNOLPHE

Go on.

AGNÈS

Then an old woman came, next day,
And found me standing in the entryway.
She said to me, "May Heaven bless you, dear,
And keep you beautiful for many a year.
God, who bestowed on you such grace and charm,
Did not intend those gifts to do men harm,
And you should know that there's a heart which bears
A wound which you've inflicted unawares."

ARNOLPHE, *aside*

Old witch! Old tool of Satan! Damn her hide!

AGNÈS

"You say I've wounded somebody?" I cried.
"Indeed you have," she said. "The victim's he
Whom yesterday you saw from the balcony."
"But how could such a thing occur?" I said;
"Can I have dropped some object on his head?"
"No," she replied, "your bright eyes dealt the blow;
Their glances are the cause of all his woe."
"Good heavens, Madam," said I in great surprise,
"Is there some dread contagion in my eyes?"
"Ah, yes, my child," said she. "Your eyes dispense,
Unwittingly, a fatal influence:
The poor young man has dwindled to a shade;
And if you cruelly deny him aid,
I greatly fear," the kind old woman went on,
"That two days more will see him dead and gone."
"Heavens," I answered, "that would be sad indeed.
But what can I do for him? What help does he need?"
"My child," said she, "he only asks of you
The privilege of a little interview;
It is your eyes alone which now can save him,
And cure him of the malady they gave him."
"If that's the case," I said, "I can't refuse;
I'll gladly see him, whenever he may choose."

ARNOLPHE, *aside*

O "kind old woman"! O vicious sorceress!
May Hell reward you for your cleverness!

49

AGNÈS

And so I saw him, which brought about his cure.
You'll grant I did the proper thing, I'm sure.
How could I have the conscience to deny
The succor he required, and let him die—
I, who so pity anyone in pain,
And cannot bear to see a chicken slain?

ARNOLPHE, *aside*

It's clear that she has meant no wrong, and I
Must blame that foolish trip I took, whereby
I left her unprotected from the lies
That rascally seducers can devise.
Oh, what if that young wretch, with one bold stroke,
Has compromised her? That would be no joke.

AGNÈS

What's wrong? You seem a trifle irritated.
Was there some harm in what I just related?

ARNOLPHE

No, but go on. I want to hear it all.
What happened when the young man came to call?

AGNÈS

Oh, if you'd seen how happy he was, how gay,
And how his sickness vanished right away,
And the jewel-case he gave me—not to forget
The coins he gave to Alain and to Georgette,
You would have loved him also, and you too—

ARNOLPHE

And when you were alone, what did he do?

AGNÈS

He swore he loved me with a matchless passion,
And said to me, in the most charming fashion,
Things which I found incomparably sweet,
And never tire of hearing him repeat,
So much do they delight my ear, and start
I know not what commotion in my heart.

ARNOLPHE, *aside*

O strange interrogation, where each reply
Makes the interrogator wish to die!
      (*To Agnès:*)
Besides these compliments, these sweet addresses,
Were there not also kisses, and caresses?

AGNÈS

Oh, yes! He took my hands, and kissed and kissed
Them both, as if he never would desist.

ARNOLPHE

And did he not take—something else as well?
      (*He notes that she is taken aback.*)
Agh!

AGNÈS

      Well, he—

[*Act Two* · *Scene Five*]

ARNOLPHE

Yes?

AGNÈS

Took—

ARNOLPHE

What?

AGNÈS

I dare not tell.
I fear that you'll be furious with me.

ARNOLPHE

No.

AGNÈS

Yes.

ARNOLPHE

No, no.

AGNÈS

Then promise not to be.

ARNOLPHE

I promise.

52

[*Act Two · Scene Five*]

AGNÈS

He took my—oh, you'll have a fit.

ARNOLPHE

No.

AGNÈS

Yes.

ARNOLPHE

No, no. The devil! Out with it!
What did he take from you?

AGNÈS

He took—

ARNOLPHE, *aside*

God save me!

AGNÈS

He took the pretty ribbon that you gave me.
Indeed, he begged so that I couldn't resist.

ARNOLPHE, *taking a deep breath*

Forget the ribbon. Tell me: once he'd kissed
Your hands, what else did he do, as you recall?

[*Act Two · Scene Five*]

AGNÈS

Does one do other things?

ARNOLPHE

            No, not at all;
But didn't he ask some further medicine
For the sad state of health that he was in?

AGNÈS

Why, no. But had he asked, you may be sure
I'd have done anything to speed his cure.

ARNOLPHE, *aside*

I've got off cheap this once, thanks be to God;
If I slip again, let all men call me clod.
    (*To Agnès:*)
Agnès, my dear, your innocence is vast;
I shan't reproach you; what is past is past.
But all that trifler wants to do—don't doubt it—
Is to deceive you, and then boast about it.

AGNÈS

Oh, no. He's often assured me otherwise.

ARNOLPHE

Ah, you don't know how that sort cheats and lies.
But do grasp this: to accept a jewel-case,
And let some coxcomb praise your pretty face,

54

And be complaisant when he takes a notion
To kiss your hands and fill you with "commotion"
Is a great sin, for which your soul could die.

AGNÈS

A sin, you say! But please, Sir, tell me why.

ARNOLPHE

Why? Why? Because, as all authority states,
It's just such deeds that Heaven abominates.

AGNÈS

Abominates! But why should Heaven feel so?
It's all so charming and so sweet, you know!
I never knew about this sort of thing
Till now, or guessed what raptures it could bring.

ARNOLPHE

Yes, all these promises of love undying,
These sighs, these kisses, are most gratifying,
But they must be enjoyed in the proper way;
One must be married first, that is to say.

AGNÈS

And once you're married, there's no evil in it?

ARNOLPHE

That's right.

AGNÈS

Oh, let me marry, then, this minute!

ARNOLPHE

If that's what you desire, I feel the same;
It was to plan your marriage that I came.

AGNÈS

What! Truly?

ARNOLPHE

Yes.

AGNÈS

How happy I shall be!

ARNOLPHE

Yes, wedded life will please you, I foresee.

AGNÈS

You really intend that we two—

ARNOLPHE

Yes, I do.

[*Act Two · Scene Five*]

 AGNÈS

Oh, how I'll kiss you if that dream comes true!

ARNOLPHE

And I'll return your kisses, every one.

AGNÈS

I'm never sure when people are making fun.
Are you quite serious?

ARNOLPHE

Yes, I'm serious. Quite.

AGNÈS

We're to be married?

ARNOLPHE

Yes.

AGNÈS

But when?

ARNOLPHE

Tonight.

[*Act Two* · *Scene Five*]

AGNÈS, *laughing*

Tonight?

ARNOLPHE

Tonight. It seems you're moved to laughter.

AGNÈS

Yes.

ARNOLPHE

Well, to see you happy is what I'm after.

AGNÈS

Oh, Sir, I owe you more than I can express!
With him, my life will be pure happiness!

ARNOLPHE

With whom?

AGNÈS

With . . . him.

ARNOLPHE

With *him!* Well, think again.
You're rather hasty in your choice of men.
It's quite another husband I have in mind;

And as for "him," as you call him, be so kind,
Regardless of his pitiable disease,
As never again to see him, if you please.
When next he calls, girl, put him in his place
By slamming the door directly in his face;
Then, if he knocks, go up and drop a brick
From the second-floor window. That should do the trick.
Do you understand, Agnès? I shall be hidden
Nearby, to see that you do as you are bidden.

AGNÈS

Oh, dear, he's so good-looking, so—

ARNOLPHE

                    Be still!

AGNÈS

I just won't have the heart—

ARNOLPHE

                    Enough; you will.
Now go upstairs.

AGNÈS

                    How can you—

ARNOLPHE

                    Do as I say.
I'm master here; I've spoken; go, obey.

SCENE ONE

ARNOLPHE, AGNÈS, ALAIN, GEORGETTE

ARNOLPHE

Yes, I'm most pleased; it couldn't have gone better.
By following my instructions to the letter,
You've put that young philanderer to flight:
See how wise generalship can set things right.
Your innocence had been abused, Agnès;
Unwittingly, you'd got into a mess,
And, lacking my good counsel, you were well
Embarked upon a course which leads to Hell.
Those beaux are all alike, believe you me:
They've ribbons, plumes, and ruffles at the knee,
Fine wigs, and polished talk, and brilliant teeth,
But they're all scales and talons underneath—
Indeed, they're devils of the vilest sort,
Who prey on women's honor for their sport.
However, owing to my watchful care,
You have emerged intact from this affair.
The firm and righteous way in which you threw
That brick at him, and dashed his hopes of you,
Persuades me that there's no cause to delay
The wedding which I promised you today.
But first, it would be well for me to make
A few remarks for your improvement's sake.
    (*To Alain, who brings a chair:*)

I'll sit here, where it's cool.
　　(*To Georgette:*) Remember, now—

GEORGETTE

Oh, Sir, we won't forget again, I vow.
That young man won't get round us any more.

ALAIN

I'll give up drink if he gets through that door.
Anyway, he's an idiot; we bit
Two coins he gave us, and they were counterfeit.

ARNOLPHE

Well, go and buy the food for supper, and then
One of you, as you're coming home again,
Can fetch the local notary from the square.
Tell him that there's a contract to prepare.

SCENE TWO

ARNOLPHE, *seated*

Agnès, stop knitting and hear what I have to say.
Lift up your head a bit, and turn this way.
    (*Putting his finger to his forehead:*)
Look at me *there* while I talk to you, right *there*,
And listen to my every word with care.
My dear, I'm going to wed you, and you should bless
Your vast good fortune and your happiness.
Reflect upon your former low estate,
And judge, then, if my goodness is not great
In raising you, a humble peasant lass,
To be a matron of the middle class,
To share the bed and the connubial bliss
Of one who's shunned the married state till this,
Withholding from a charming score or two
The honor which he now bestows on you.
Be ever mindful, Agnès, that you would be,
Without this union, a nonentity;
And let that thought incline your heart to merit
The name which I shall lend you, and to bear it
With such propriety that I shall never
Regret my choice for any cause whatever.
Marriage, Agnès, is no light matter; the role
Of wife requires austerity of soul,

65

And I do not exalt you to that station
To lead a life of heedless dissipation.
Yours is the weaker sex, please realize;
It is the beard in which all power lies,
And though there are two portions of mankind,
Those portions are not equal, you will find:
One half commands, the other must obey;
The second serves the first in every way;
And that obedience which the soldier owes
His general, or the loyal servant shows
His master, or the good child pays his sire,
Or the stern abbot looks for in the friar,
Is nothing to the pure docility,
The deep submission and humility
Which a good wife must ever exhibit toward
The man who is her master, chief, and lord.
Should he regard her with a serious air,
She must avert her eyes, and never dare
To lift them to his face again, unless
His look should change to one of tenderness.
Such things aren't understood by women today,
But don't let bad example lead you astray.
Don't emulate those flirts whose indiscretions
Are told all over town at gossip-sessions,
Or yield to Satan's trickery by allowing
Young fops to please you with their smiles and bowing.
Remember that, in marrying, I confide
To you, Agnès, my honor and my pride;
That honor is a tender, fragile thing
With which there can be no light dallying;
And that all misbehaving wives shall dwell
In ever-boiling cauldrons down in Hell.
These are no idle lessons which I impart,
And you'll do well to get them all by heart.

Your soul, if you observe them, and abjure
Flirtation, will be lily-white and pure;
But deviate from honor, and your soul
Will forthwith grow as vile and black as coal;
All will abhor you as a thing of evil,
Till one day you'll be taken by the Devil,
And Hell's eternal fire is where he'll send you—
From which sad fate may Heaven's grace defend you.
Make me a curtsey. Now then, just as a novice,
Entering the convent, learns by heart her office,
So, entering wedlock, you should do the same.
                    (*He rises.*)
I have, in my pocket, a book of no small fame
From which you'll learn the office of a wife.
'T was written by some man of pious life.
Study his teaching faithfully, and heed it.
Here, take the book; let's hear how well you read it.

AGNÈS, *reading*

The Maxims of Marriage
or
The Duties of a Married Woman,
Together with Her Daily Exercises.

First Maxim:
A woman who in church has said
  She'll love and honor and obey
Should get it firmly in her head,
  Despite the fashions of the day,
That he who took her for his own
Has taken her for his bed alone.

ARNOLPHE

I shall explain that; doubtless you're perplexed.
But, for the present, let us hear what's next.

AGNÈS, *continuing*

Second Maxim:

She needs no fine attire
More than he may desire
Who is her lord and master.
To dress for any taste but his is vain;
If others find her plain,
'T is no disaster.

Third Maxim:

Let her not daub her face
With paint and patch and powder-base
And creams which promise beauty on the label.
It is not for their husbands' sake
But vanity's, that women undertake
The labors of the dressing table.

Fourth Maxim:

Let her be veiled whenever she leaves the house,
So that her features are obscure and dim.
If she desires to please her spouse,
She must please no one else but him.

Fifth Maxim:

Except for friends who call
To see her husband, let her not admit
Anyone at all.

68

A visitor whose end
Is to amuse the wife with gallant wit
    Is *not* the husband's friend.

Sixth Maxim:

To men who would confer kind gifts upon her,
She must reply with self-respecting nays.
Not to refuse would be to court dishonor.
Nothing is given for nothing nowadays.

Seventh Maxim:

She has no need, whatever she may think,
Of writing table, paper, pen, or ink.
In a proper house, the husband is the one
To do whatever writing's to be done.

Eighth Maxim:

    At those licentious things
    Called social gatherings,
Wives are corrupted by the worldly crowd.
Since, at such functions, amorous plots are laid
    And married men betrayed,
    They should not be allowed.

Ninth Maxim:

Let the wise wife, who cares for her good name,
Decline to play at any gambling game.
In such seductive pastimes wives can lose
Far more than coins, or bills, or I.O.U.'s.

Tenth Maxim:

    It is not good for wives
    To go on gay excursions,
    Picnics, or country drives.

In all such light diversions,
No matter who's the host,
The husbands pay the most.

Eleventh Maxim—

ARNOLPHE

Good. Read the rest to yourself. I'll clarify
Whatever may confuse you, by and by.
I've just recalled some business I'd forgot;
'T will only take a moment, like as not.
Go in, and treat that precious book with care.
If the notary comes, tell him to have a chair.

SCENE THREE

ARNOLPHE

What could be safer than to marry her?
She'll do and be whatever I prefer.
She's like a lump of wax, and I can mold her
Into what shape I like, as she grows older.
True, she was almost lured away from me,
Whilst I was gone, through her simplicity;
But if one's wife must have some imperfection,
It's best that she should err in that direction.
Such faults as hers are easy to remove:
A simple wife is eager to improve,
And if she has been led astray, a slight
Admonitory talk will set her right.
But a clever wife's another kettle of fish:
One's at the mercy of her every wish;
What she desires, she'll have at any cost,
And reasoning with her is labor lost.
Her wicked wit makes virtues of her crimes,
Makes mock of principle, and oftentimes
Contrives, in furtherance of some wicked plan,
Intrigues which can defeat the shrewdest man.
Against her there is no defense, for she's
Unbeatable at plots and strategies,
And once she has resolved to amputate
Her husband's honor, he must bow to fate.

71

There's many a decent man could tell that story.
But that young fool will have no chance to glory
In my disgrace: he has too loose a tongue,
And that's a fault of Frenchmen, old or young.
When they are lucky in a love affair,
To keep the secret's more than they can bear;
A foolish vanity torments them, till
They'd rather hang, by Heaven, than be still.
What but the spells of Satan could incline
Women to favor men so asinine?
But here he comes; my feelings must not show
As I extract from him his tale of woe.

SCENE FOUR

HORACE, ARNOLPHE

HORACE

I've just been at your house, and I begin
To fear I'm fated never to find you in.
But I'll persist, and one day have the joy—

ARNOLPHE

Ah, come, no idle compliments, my boy.
All this fine talk, so flowery and so polished,
Is something I'd be glad to see abolished.
It's a vile custom: most men waste two-thirds
Of every day exchanging empty words.
Let's put our hats on, now, and be at ease.
Well, how's your love life going? Do tell me, please.
I was a bit distrait when last we met,
But what you told me I did not forget:
Your bold beginnings left me much impressed,
And now I'm all agog to hear the rest.

HORACE

Since I unlocked my heart to you, alas,
My hopes have come to an unhappy pass.

ARNOLPHE

Oh, dear! How so?

HORACE

Just now—alas—I learned
That my beloved's guardian has returned.

ARNOLPHE

That's bad.

HORACE

What's more, he's well aware that we've
Been meeting secretly, without his leave.

ARNOLPHE

But how could he so quickly find that out?

HORACE

I don't know, but he has, beyond a doubt.
I went at my usual hour, more or less,
To pay my homage to her loveliness,
And found the servants changed in attitude.
They barred my way; their words and looks were rude.
"Be off!" they told me, and with no good grace
They slammed the door directly in my face.

ARNOLPHE

Right in your face!

HORACE

Yes.

ARNOLPHE

Dreadful. Tell me more.

HORACE

I tried to reason with them through the door,
But whatsoever I said to them, they cried,
"The master says you're not to come inside."

ARNOLPHE

They wouldn't open it?

HORACE

No. And then Agnès,
On orders from her guardian, as one could guess,
Came to her window, said that she was sick
Of my attentions, and threw down a brick.

ARNOLPHE

A brick, you say!

HORACE

A brick; and it wasn't small.
Not what one hopes for when one pays a call.

ARNOLPHE

Confound it! That's no mild rebuff, my lad.
I fear your situation's pretty bad.

HORACE

Yes, that old fool's return has spoiled my game.

ARNOLPHE

You have my deepest sympathy; it's a shame.

HORACE

He's wrecked my plans.

ARNOLPHE

        Oh, come; you've lost some
              ground,
But some means of recouping will be found.

HORACE

With a little inside help, I might by chance
Outwit this jealous fellow's vigilance.

ARNOLPHE

That should be easy. The lady, as you say,
Loves you.

76

HORACE

Indeed, yes.

ARNOLPHE

Then you'll find a way.

HORACE

I hope so.

ARNOLPHE

You must not be put to flight
By that ungracious brick.

HORACE

Of course you're right.
I knew at once that that old fool was back
And secretly directing the attack.
But what amazed me (you'll be amazed as well)
Was something else she did, of which I'll tell—
A daring trick one wouldn't expect to see
Played by a girl of such simplicity.
Love is indeed a wondrous master, Sir,
Whose teaching makes us what we never were,
And under whose miraculous tuition
One suddenly can change one's disposition.
It overturns our settled inclinations,
Causing the most astounding transformations:
The miser's made a spendthrift overnight,
The coward valiant, and the boor polite;

77

Love spurs the sluggard on to high endeavor,
And moves the artless maiden to be clever.
Well, such a miracle has changed Agnès.
She cried, just now, with seeming bitterness,
"Go! I refuse to see you, and don't ask why;
To all your questions, here is my reply!"—
And having made that statement, down she threw
The brick I've mentioned, and a letter, too.
Note how her words apply to brick *and* letter:
Isn't that fine? Could any ruse be better?
Aren't you amazed? Do you see what great effect
True love can have upon the intellect?
Can you deny its power to inspire
The gentlest heart with fortitude and fire?
How do you like that trick with the letter, eh?
A most astute young woman, wouldn't you say?
As for my jealous rival, isn't the role
He's played in this affair extremely droll?
Well?

ARNOLPHE

Yes, quite droll.

HORACE

       Well, laugh, if that's the case!
(*Arnolphe gives a forced laugh.*)
My, what a fool! He fortifies his place
Against me, using bricks for cannon balls,
As if he feared that I might storm the walls;
What's more, in his anxiety he rallies
His two domestics to repulse my sallies;
And then he's hoodwinked by the girl he meant

To keep forever meek and innocent!
I must confess that, though this silly man's
Return to town has balked my amorous plans,
The whole thing's been so comical that I find
That I'm convulsed whenever it comes to mind.
You haven't laughed as much as I thought you would.

ARNOLPHE, *with a forced laugh*

I beg your pardon; I've done the best I could.

HORACE

But let me show you the letter she wrote, my friend.
What her heart feels, her artless hand has penned
In the most touching terms, the sweetest way,
With pure affection, purest naïveté;
Nature herself, I think, would so express
Love's first awakening and its sweet distress.

ARNOLPHE, *aside*

Behold what scribbling leads to! It was quite
Against my wishes that she learned to write.

HORACE, *reading*

I am moved to write to you, but I am much at a loss
as to how to begin. I have thoughts which I should like
you to know of; but I don't know how to go about telling
them to you, and I mistrust my own words. I begin to
perceive that I have always been kept in a state of ignorance, and so I am fearful of writing something I
shouldn't, or of saying more than I ought. In truth, I

don't know what you have done to me, but I know that
I am mortally vexed by the harsh things I am made to do
to you, that it will be the most painful thing in the world
to give you up, and that I would be happy indeed to be
yours. Perhaps it is rash of me to say that; but in any case
I cannot help saying it, and I wish that I could have my
desire without doing anything wrong. I am constantly
told that all young men are deceivers, that they mustn't
be listened to, and that all you have said to me is mere
trickery; I assure you, however, that I have not yet been
able to think that of you, and your words so touch me
that I cannot believe them false. Please tell me frankly
what you intend; for truly, since my own intentions are
blameless, it would be very wicked of you to deceive me,
and I think that I should die of despair.

ARNOLPHE, *aside*

The bitch!

HORACE

What's wrong?

ARNOLPHE

Oh, nothing: I was sneezing.

HORACE

Was ever a style so amiable, so pleasing?
Despite the tyranny she's had to bear,
Isn't her nature sweet beyond compare?
And is it not a crime of the basest kind

For anyone to stifle such a mind,
To starve so fine a spirit, and to enshroud
In ignorance a soul so well-endowed?
Love has begun to waken her, however,
And if some kind star favors my endeavor
I'll free her from that utter beast, that black
Villain, that wretch, that brute, that maniac—

ARNOLPHE

Good-bye.

HORACE

What, going?

ARNOLPHE

I've just recalled that I'm
Due somewhere else in a few minutes' time.

HORACE

Wait! Can you think of someone who might possess
An entrée to that house, and to Agnès?
I hate to trouble you, but do please lend
Whatever help you can, as friend to friend.
The servants, as I said, both man and maid,
Have turned against my cause, and can't be swayed.
Just now, despite my every blandishment,
They eyed me coldly, and would not relent.
I had, for a time, the aid of an old woman
Whose talent for intrigue was superhuman;
She served me, at the start, with much success,

81

But died four days ago, to my distress.
Don't you know someone who could help me out?

ARNOLPHE

I don't; but you'll find someone, I don't doubt.

HORACE

Farewell, then, Sir. You'll be discreet, I know.

SCENE FIVE

ARNOLPHE

ARNOLPHE

In that boy's presence, what hell I undergo,
Trying to hide my anguish from his eye!
To think that an innocent girl should prove so sly!
Either she's fooled me, and never *was* naïve,
Or Satan's just now taught her to deceive.
That cursèd letter! I wish that I were dead.
Plainly that callow wretch has turned her head,
Captured her mind and heart, eclipsed me there,
And doomed me to distraction and despair.
The loss of her entails a double hell:
My honor suffers, and my love as well.
It drives me mad to see myself displaced,
And all my careful planning gone to waste.
To be revenged on her, I need but wait
And let her giddy passion meet its fate;
The upshot can't be anything but bad.
But oh, to lose the thing one loves is sad.
Good Lord! To rear her with such calculation,
And then fall victim to infatuation!
She has no funds, no family, yet she can dare
Abuse my lavish kindness and my care;
And what, for Heaven's sake, is my reaction?
In spite of all, I love her to distraction!
Have you no shame, fool? Don't you resent her crimes?

Oh, I could slap my face a thousand times!
I'll go inside for a bit, but only to see
How she will face me after her treachery.
Kind Heaven, let no dishonor stain my brow;
Or if it is decreed that I must bow
To that misfortune, lend me at least, I pray,
Such patient strength as some poor men display.

SCENE ONE

ARNOLPHE

ARNOLPHE, *entering from the house, alone*

I can't hold still a minute, I declare.
My anxious thoughts keep darting here and there,
Planning defenses, seeking to prevent
That rascal from achieving his intent.
How calm the traitress looked when I went in!
Despite her crimes, she shows no sense of sin,
And though she's all but sent me to my grave,
How like a little saint she dares behave!
The more she sat there, cool and unperturbed,
The less I thought my fury could be curbed;
Yet, strange to say, my heart's increasing ire
Seemed only to redouble my desire.
I was embittered, desperate, irate,
And yet her beauty had never seemed so great.
Never did her bright eyes so penetrate me,
So rouse my spirit, so infatuate me;
Oh, it would break the heart within my breast
Should fate subject me to this cruel jest.
What! Have I supervised her education
With loving care and long consideration,
Sheltered her since she was a tiny creature,
Cherished sweet expectations for her future,
For thirteen years molded her character
And based my hopes of happiness on her,

87

Only to see some young fool steal the prize
Of her affection, under my very eyes,
And just when she and I were all but wed?
Ah, no, young friend! Ah, no, young chucklehead!
I mean to stop you; I swear that you shall not
Succeed, however well you scheme and plot,
And that you'll have no cause to laugh at me.

SCENE TWO

THE NOTARY, ARNOLPHE

NOTARY

Ah, here you are, Sir! I am the notary.
So, there's a contract which you'd have me draw?

ARNOLPHE, *unaware of the notary*

How shall I do it?

NOTARY

According to the law.

ARNOLPHE, *still oblivious*

I must be prudent, and think what course is best.

NOTARY

I shall do nothing against your interest.

ARNOLPHE, *oblivious*

One must anticipate the unexpected.

NOTARY

In my hands, you'll be thoroughly protected.
But do remember, lest you be betrayed,
To sign no contract till the dowry's paid.

ARNOLPHE, *oblivious*

I must act covertly; if this thing gets out,
The gossips will have much to blab about.

NOTARY

If you're so anxious not to make a stir,
The contract can be drawn in secret, Sir.

ARNOLPHE, *oblivious*

But how shall she be dealt with? Can I condone—

NOTARY

The dowry is proportional to her own.

ARNOLPHE, *oblivious*

It's hard to be strict with one whom you adore.

NOTARY

In that case, you may wish to give her more.

ARNOLPHE, *oblivious*

How should I treat the girl? I must decide.

90

[*Act Four · Scene Two*]

NOTARY

As a general rule, the husband gives the bride
A dowry that's one-third the size of hers;
But he may increase the sum, if he prefers.

ARNOLPHE, *oblivious*

If—

NOTARY, *Arnolphe now noticing him*

As for property, and its division
In case of death, the husband makes provision
As he thinks best.

ARNOLPHE

Eh?

NOTARY

He can make certain of
His bride's security, and show his love,
By jointure, or a settlement whereby
The gift is canceled should the lady die,
Reverting to her heirs, if so agreed;
Or go by common law; or have a deed
Of gift appended to the instrument,
Either by his sole wish, or by consent.
Why shrug your shoulders? Am I talking rot?
Do I know contracts, Sir, or do I not?
Who could instruct me? Who would be so bold?
Do I not know that spouses jointly hold

91

Goods, chattels, lands, and money in their two names,
Unless one party should renounce all claims?
Do I not know that a third of the bride's resources
Enters the joint estate—

ARNOLPHE

All that, of course, is
True. But who asked for all this pedantry?

NOTARY

You did! And now you sniff and shrug at me,
And treat my competence with ridicule.

ARNOLPHE

The devil take this ugly-featured fool!
Good day, good day. An end to all this chatter.

NOTARY

Did you not ask my aid in a legal matter?

ARNOLPHE

Yes, yes, but now the matter's been deferred.
When your advice is needed, I'll send word.
Meanwhile, stop blathering, you blatherskite!

NOTARY

He's mad, I judge; and I think my judgment's right.

SCENE THREE

THE NOTARY, ALAIN, GEORGETTE, ARNOLPHE

NOTARY, *to Alain and Georgette*

Your master sent you to fetch me, isn't that so?

ALAIN

Yes.

NOTARY

How you feel about him I don't know,
But I regard him as a senseless boor.
Tell him I said so.

GEORGETTE

We will, you may be sure.

SCENE FOUR

ALAIN, GEORGETTE, ARNOLPHE

ALAIN

Sir—

ARNOLPHE

    Ah, come here, my good friends, tried and true:
You've amply proved that I may count on you.

ALAIN

The notary—

ARNOLPHE

        Tell me later, will you not?
My honor's threatened by a vicious plot;
Think, children, what distress you'd feel, what shame,
If some dishonor touched your master's name!
You wouldn't dare to leave the house, for fear
That all the town would point at you, and sneer.
Since we're together, then, in this affair,
You must be ever watchful, and take care
That no approach that gallant may adopt—

94

[*Act Four · Scene Four*]

GEORGETTE

We've learned our lesson, Sir; he shall be stopped.

ARNOLPHE

Beware his fine words and his flatteries.

ALAIN

Of course.

GEORGETTE

We can resist such talk with ease.

ARNOLPHE, *to Alain*

What if he said, "Alain, for mercy's sake,
Do me a kindness"—what answer would you make?

ALAIN

I'd say, "You fool!"

ARNOLPHE

Good, good. (*To Georgette:*)
"Georgette, my dear,
I'm sure you're just as sweet as you appear."

GEORGETTE

"Fathead!"

[*Act Four · Scene Four*]

ARNOLPHE

Good, good. (*To Alain:*) "Come, let me in.
You know
That my intent is pure as the driven snow."

ALAIN

"Sir, you're a knave!"

ARNOLPHE

Well said. (*To Georgette:*) "Unless you take
Pity on my poor heart, it's sure to break."

GEORGETTE

"You are an impudent ass!"

ARNOLPHE

Well said, Georgette.
"I'm not the sort of person to forget
A favor, or begrudge the *quid pro quo*,
As these few coins, Alain, will serve to show.
And you, Georgette, take this and buy a dress.
        (*Both hold out their hands and take the money.*)
That's but a specimen of my largesse.
And all I ask is that you grant to me
An hour of your young mistress' company."

GEORGETTE, *giving him a shove*

"You're crazy!"

[*Act Four · Scene Four*]

ARNOLPHE

Good!

ALAIN, *shoving Arnolphe*

"Move on!"

ARNOLPHE

Good!

GEORGETTE, *shoving Arnolphe*

"Out of my
sight!"

ARNOLPHE

Good, good—but that's enough.

GEORGETTE

Did I do it right?

ALAIN

Is that how we're to treat him?

ARNOLPHE

You were fine;
Except for the money, which you should decline.

[*Act Four · Scene Four*]

GEORGETTE

We didn't think, Sir. That was wrong indeed.

ALAIN

Would you like to do it over again?

ARNOLPHE

                     No need;
Go back inside.

ALAIN

       Sir, if you say the word, we—

ARNOLPHE

No, that will do; go in at once; you heard me.
Just keep the money; I shall be with you shortly.
Be on your guard, and ready to support me.

SCENE FIVE

ARNOLPHE

ARNOLPHE

The cobbler at the corner is sharp of eye;
I think that I'll enlist him as a spy.
As for Agnès, I'll keep her under guard,
And all dishonest women shall be barred—
Hairdressers, glovers, handkerchief-makers, those
Who come to the door with ribbons, pins, and bows,
And often, as a sideline to such wares,
Are go-betweens in secret love affairs.
I know the world, and the tricks that people use;
That boy will have to invent some brand-new ruse
If he's to get a message in to her.

SCENE SIX

HORACE, ARNOLPHE

HORACE

What luck to find you in this quarter, Sir!
I've just had a narrow escape, believe you me!
Just after I left you, whom did I chance to see
Upon her shady balcony, but the fair
Agnès, who had come out to take the air!
She managed, having signaled me to wait,
To steal downstairs and open the garden gate.
We went to her room, and were no sooner there
Than we heard her jealous guardian on the stair;
In which great peril I was thrust by her
Into a wardrobe where her dresses were.
He entered. I couldn't see him, but I heard
Him striding back and forth without a word,
Heaving deep sighs of woe again and again,
Pounding upon the tables now and then,
Kicking a little dog, who yipped in fright,
And throwing her possessions left and right.
What's more, to give his fury full release,
He knocked two vases off her mantelpiece.
Clearly the old goat had some vague, dismaying
Sense of the tricks his captive had been playing.
At last, when all his anger had been spent
On objects which were dumb and innocent,
The frantic man, without a word, went striding

100

Out of the room, and I came out of hiding.
Quite naturally, we didn't dare extend
Our rendezvous, because our jealous friend
Was still about; tonight, however, I
Shall visit her, quite late, and on the sly.
Our plan is this: I'll cough, three times, outside;
At that, the window will be opened wide;
Then, with a ladder and the assistance of
Agnès, I'll climb into our bower of love.
Since you're my only friend, I tell you this—
For telling, as you know, augments one's bliss.
However vast the joy, one must confide
In someone else before one's satisfied.
You share, I know, my happy expectations.
But now, farewell; I must make preparations.

SCENE SEVEN

ARNOLPHE

The evil star that's hounding me to death
Gives me no time in which to catch my breath!
Must I, again and again, be forced to see
My measures foiled through their complicity?
Shall I, at my ripe age, be duped, forsooth,
By a green girl and by a harebrained youth?
For twenty years I've sagely contemplated
The woeful lives of men unwisely mated,
And analyzed with care the slips whereby
The best-planned marriages have gone awry;
Thus schooled by others' failures, I felt that I'd
Be able, when I chose to take a bride,
To ward off all mischance, and be protected
From griefs to which so many are subjected.
I took, to that end, all the shrewd and wise
Precautions which experience could devise;
Yet, as if fate had made the stern decision
That no man living should escape derision,
I find, for all my pondering of this
Great matter, all my keen analysis,
The twenty years and more which I have spent
In planning to escape the embarrassment
So many husbands suffer from today,
That I'm as badly victimized as they.

But no, damned fate, I challenge your decree!
The lovely prize is in my custody,
And though her heart's been filched by that young pest,
I guarantee that he'll not get the rest,
And that this evening's gallant rendezvous
Won't go as smoothly as they'd like it to.
There's one good thing about my present fix—
That I'm forewarned of all my rival's tricks,
And that this oaf who's aiming to undo me
Confesses all his bad intentions to me.

SCENE EIGHT

CHRYSALDE, ARNOLPHE

CHRYSALDE

Well, shall we dine, and then go out for a stroll?

ARNOLPHE

No, no, the dinner's off.

CHRYSALDE

Well, well, how droll!

ARNOLPHE

Forgive me: there's a crisis I must face.

CHRYSALDE

Your wedding plans have changed? Is that the case?

ARNOLPHE

I have no need of your solicitude.

CHRYSALDE

Tell me your troubles, now, and don't be rude.
I'd guess, friend, that your marriage scheme has met
With difficulties, and that you're upset.
To judge by your expression, I'd almost swear it.

ARNOLPHE

Whatever happens, I shall have the merit
Of not resembling some in this community,
Who let young gallants cheat them with impunity.

CHRYSALDE

It's odd that you, with your good intellect,
Are so obsessive in this one respect,
Measure all happiness thereby, and base
On it alone men's honor or disgrace.
Greed, envy, vice, and cowardice are not
Important sins to you; the one grave blot
You find on any scutcheon seems to be
The crime of having suffered cuckoldry.
Now, come: shall a man be robbed of his good name
Through an ill chance for which he's not to blame?
Shall a good husband lacerate his soul
With guilt for matters not in his control?
When a man marries, why must we scorn or praise him
According to whether or not his wife betrays him?
And if she does so, why must her husband see
The fact as an immense catastrophe?
Do realize that, to a man of sense,
There's nothing crushing in such accidents;
That, since no man can dodge the blows of fate,

One's sense of failure should not be too great,
And that there's no harm done, whatever they say,
If one but takes things in the proper way.
In difficulties of this sort, it seems,
As always, wiser to avoid extremes.
One shouldn't ape those husbands who permit
Such scandal, and who take a pride in it,
Dropping the names of their wives' latest gallants,
Praising their persons, bragging of their talents,
Professing warm regard for them, attending
The parties that they give, and so offending
Society, which properly resents
Displays of laxity and impudence.
Needless to say, such conduct will not do;
And yet the other extreme's improper too.
If men do wrong to flatter their wives' gallants,
It's no less bad when, lacking tact and balance,
They vent their grievances with savage fury,
Calling the whole world to be judge and jury,
And won't be satisfied till they acquaint
All ears whatever with their loud complaint.
Between these two extremes, my friend, there lies
A middle way that's favored by the wise,
And which, if followed, will preserve one's face
However much one's wife may court disgrace.
In short, then, cuckoldry need not be dreaded
Like some dire monster, fierce and many-headed;
It can be lived with, if one has the wit
To take it calmly, and make the best of it.

ARNOLPHE

For that fine speech, the great fraternity
Of cuckolds owes you thanks, your Excellency;

106

And all men, if they heard your wisdom, would
Make joyous haste to join the brotherhood.

CHRYSALDE

No, that I shouldn't approve. But since it's fate
Whereby we're joined to one or another mate,
One should take marriage as one takes picquette,
In which, if one has made a losing bet,
One takes the setback calmly, and takes pains
To do the best one can with what remains.

ARNOLPHE

In other words, eat hearty and sleep tight,
And tell yourself that everything's all right.

CHRYSALDE

Laugh on, my friend; but I can, in all sobriety,
Name fifty things which cause me more anxiety,
And would, if they occurred, appall me more
Than this misfortune which you so abhor.
Had I to choose between adversities,
I'd rather be a cuckold, if you please,
Than marry one of those good wives who find
Continual reason to upbraid mankind,
Those virtuous shrews, those fiendish paragons,
As violently chaste as Amazons,
Who, having had the goodness not to horn us,
Accord themselves the right to nag and scorn us,
And make us pay for their fidelity
By being as vexatious as can be.
Do learn, friend, that when all is said and done,

Cuckoldry's what you make of it; that one
Might welcome it in certain situations,
And that, like all things, it has compensations.

ARNOLPHE

Well, if you want it, may you get your wish;
But, as for me, it's not at all my dish.
Before I'd let my brow be decked with horn—

CHRYSALDE

Tut, tut! Don't swear, or you may be forsworn.
If fate has willed it, your resolves will fail,
And all your oaths will be of no avail.

ARNOLPHE

I! I a cuckold?

CHRYSALDE

Don't let it fret you so.
It happens to the best of men, you know.
Cuckolds exist with whom, if I may be frank,
You can't compare for person, wealth, or rank.

ARNOLPHE

I have no wish to be compared with such.
Enough, now, of your mockery; it's too much.
You try my patience.

CHRYSALDE

So, you're annoyed with me?
Ah, well. Good-bye. But bear in mind that he
Who thumps his chest and swears upon his soul
That he will never play the cuckold's role
Is studying for the part, and may well get it.

ARNOLPHE

That won't occur, I swear; I shall not let it.
I shall remove that threat this very minute.
(*He knocks at his own gate.*)

SCENE NINE

ARNOLPHE

My friends, the battle's joined, and we must win it.
Your love for me, by which I'm touched and moved,
Must now, in this emergency, be proved,
And if your deeds repay my confidence,
You may expect a handsome recompense.
This very night—don't tell a soul, my friends—
A certain rascal whom you know intends
To scale the wall and see Agnès; but we
Shall lay a little trap for him, we three.
You'll both be armed with clubs, and when the young
Villain has almost reached the topmost rung
(I meanwhile shall have flung the shutters wide),
You shall lean out and so lambaste his hide,
So bruise his ribs by your combined attack,
That he will never dream of coming back.
Don't speak my name while this is happening, mind you,
Or let him know that I am there behind you.
Have you the pluck to serve me in this action?

ALAIN

If blows are called for, we can give satisfaction.
I'll show you that this good right arm's not lame.

[*Act Four · Scene Nine*]

GEORGETTE

Mine looks less strong than his, but all the same
Our foe will know that he's been beaten by it.

ARNOLPHE

Go in, then; and, whatever you do, keep quiet.
                (*Alone:*)
Tonight, I'll give a lesson to mankind.
If all endangered husbands took a mind
To greet their wives' intrusive gallants thus,
Cuckolds, I think, would be less numerous.

SCENE ONE

ALAIN, GEORGETTE, ARNOLPHE

ARNOLPHE

You brutes! What made you be so heavy-handed?

ALAIN

But, Sir, we only did as you commanded.

ARNOLPHE

Don't put the blame on me; your guilt is plain.
I wished him beaten; I didn't wish him slain.
And furthermore, if you'll recall, I said
To hit him on the ribs, not on the head.
It's a ghastly situation in which I'm placed;
How is this young man's murder to be faced?
Go in, now, and be silent as the grave
About that innocent command I gave.
                    (*Alone:*)
It's nearly daybreak. I must take thought, and see
How best to cope with this dire tragedy.
God help me! What will the boy's father say
When this appalling story comes his way?

SCENE TWO

HORACE

Who's this, I wonder. I'd best approach with care.

ARNOLPHE

How could I have foreseen . . . I say, who's there?

HORACE

Seigneur Arnolphe?

ARNOLPHE

        Yes—

HORACE

                It's Horace, once more.
My, you're up early! I was heading for
Your house, to ask a favor.

ARNOLPHE

                Oh, God, I'm dizzy.
Is he a vision? Is he a ghost? What is he?

HORACE

Sir, I'm in trouble once again, I fear.
It's providential that you should appear
Just at the moment when your help was needed.
My plans, I'm happy to tell you, have succeeded
Beyond all expectations, and despite
An incident which might have spoiled them quite.
I don't know how it happened, but someone knew
About our contemplated rendezvous;
For, just as I'd almost reached her window sill,
I saw some frightful figures, armed to kill,
Lean out above me, waving their clubs around.
I lost my footing, tumbled to the ground,
And thus, though rather scratched and bruised, was spared
The thumping welcome which they had prepared.
Those brutes (of whom Old Jealous, I suppose,
Was one) ascribed my tumble to their blows,
And since I lay there, motionless, in the dirt
For several minutes, being stunned and hurt,
They judged that they had killed me, and they all
Took fright at that, and so began to brawl.
I lay in silence, hearing their angry cries:
They blamed each other for my sad demise,
Then tiptoed out, in darkness and in dread,
To feel my body, and see if I were dead.
As you can well imagine, I played the part
Of a limp, broken corpse with all my heart.
Quite overcome with terror, they withdrew,
And I was thinking of withdrawing, too,
When young Agnès came hurrying, out of breath
And much dismayed by my supposèd death:
She had been able, of course, to overhear
All that my foes had babbled in their fear,

And while they were distracted and unnerved
She'd slipped from the house, entirely unobserved.
Ah, how she wept with happiness when she found
That I was, after all, both safe and sound!
Well, to be brief: electing to be guided
By her own heart, the charming girl decided
Not to return to her guardian, but to flee,
Entrusting her security to me.
What must his tyranny be, if it can force
So shy a girl to take so bold a course!
And think what peril she might thus incur,
If I were capable of wronging her.
Ah, but my love's too pure for that, too strong;
I'd rather die than do her any wrong;
So admirable is she that all I crave
Is to be with her even to the grave.
I know my father: this will much displease him,
But we shall manage somehow to appease him.
In any case, she's won my heart, and I
Could not desert her, even if I chose to try.
The favor I ask of you is rather large:
It's that you take my darling in your charge,
And keep her, if you will, for several days
In your own house, concealed from the world's gaze.
I ask your help in this because I'm bent
On throwing all pursuers off the scent;
Also because, if she were seen with me,
There might be talk of impropriety.
To you, my loyal friend, I've dared to impart,
Without reserve, the secrets of my heart,
And likewise it's to you I now confide
My dearest treasure and my future bride.

[*Act Five · Scene Two*]

ARNOLPHE

I'm at your service; on that you may depend.

HORACE

You'll grant the favor that I ask, dear friend?

ARNOLPHE

Of course; most willingly. I'm glad indeed
That I can help you in your hour of need.
Thank Heaven that you asked me! There's no request
To which I could accede with greater zest.

HORACE

How kind you are! What gratitude I feel!
I feared you might refuse my rash appeal;
But you're a man of the world, urbane and wise,
Who looks upon young love with tolerant eyes.
My man is guarding her, just down the street.

ARNOLPHE

It's almost daylight. Where had we better meet?
Someone might see me, if you brought her here,
And should you bring her to my house, I fear
'T would start the servants talking. We must look
For some more shadowy and secluded nook.
That garden's handy; I shall await her there.

[*Act Five · Scene Two*]

HORACE

You're right, Sir. We must act with the utmost care.
I'll go, and quickly bring Agnès to you,
Then seek my lodgings without more ado.

ARNOLPHE, *alone*

Ah, Fortune! This good turn will compensate
For all the tricks you've played on me of late.
(*He hides his face in his cloak.*)

SCENE THREE

AGNÈS, HORACE, ARNOLPHE

HORACE

Just come with me; there's no cause for alarm.
I'm taking you where you'll be safe from harm.
To stay together would be suicide:
Go in, and let this gentleman be your guide.
> (*Arnolphe, whom she does not recognize,*
> *takes her hand.*)

AGNÈS

Why are you leaving me?

HORACE

Dear Agnès, I must.

AGNÈS

You'll very soon be coming back, I trust?

HORACE

I shall; my yearning heart will see to that.

[*Act Five · Scene Three*]

AGNÈS

Without you, life is miserable and flat.

HORACE

When I'm away from you, I pine and grieve.

AGNÈS

Alas! If that were so, you wouldn't leave.

HORACE

You know how strong my love is, and how true.

AGNÈS

Ah, no, you don't love me as I love you.
    (*Arnolphe tugs at her hand.*)
Why does he pull my hand?

HORACE

              'T would ruin us,
My dear, if we were seen together thus,
And therefore this true friend, who's filled with worry
About our welfare, urges you to hurry.

AGNÈS

But why must I go with him—a perfect stranger?

[*Act Five · Scene Three*]

HORACE

Don't fret. In his hands you'll be out of danger.

AGNÈS

I'd rather be in *your* hands; that was why—
       (*To Arnolphe, who tugs her hand again:*)
Wait, wait.

HORACE

It's daybreak. I must go. Good-bye.

AGNÈS

When shall I see you?

HORACE

Very soon, I swear.

AGNÈS

Till that sweet moment, I'll be in despair.

HORACE, *leaving, to himself*

My happiness is assured; my fears may cease;
Praise be to Heaven, I now can sleep in peace.

SCENE FOUR

ARNOLPHE, AGNÈS

ARNOLPHE, *hiding his face in his cloak, and
disguising his voice*

Come, this is not where you're to stay, my child;
It's elsewhere that you shall be domiciled.
You're going to a safe, sequestered place.
    (*Revealing himself, and using his normal voice:*)
Do you know me?

AGNÈS, *recognizing him*

    Aagh!

ARNOLPHE

             You wicked girl! My face
Would seem, just now, to give you rather a fright.
Oh, clearly I'm a most unwelcome sight:
I interfere with your romantic plan.
    (*Agnès turns and looks in vain for Horace.*)
No use to look for help from that young man;
He couldn't hear you now; he's gone too far.
Well, well! For one so young, how sly you are!
You ask—most innocently, it would appear—
If children are begotten through the ear,
Yet you know all too well, I now discover,

How to keep trysts—at midnight—with a lover!
What honeyed words you spoke to him just now!
Who taught you such beguilements? Tell me how,
Within so short a time, you've learned so much!
You used to be afraid of ghosts and such:
Has your gallant taught you not to fear the night?
You ingrate! To deceive me so, despite
The loving care with which you have been blessed!
Oh, I have warmed a serpent at my breast
Until, reviving, it unkindly bit
The very hand that was caressing it!

AGNÈS

Why are you cross with me?

ARNOLPHE

Oh! So I'm unfair?

AGNÈS

I've done no wrong of which I am aware.

ARNOLPHE

Was it right, then, to run off with that young beau?

AGNÈS

He wants me for his wife; he's told me so.
I've only done as you advised; you said
That, so as not to sin, one ought to wed.

125

ARNOLPHE

Yes, but I made it perfectly clear that I'd
Resolved, myself, to take you as my bride.

AGNÈS

Yes; but if I may give my point of view,
He'd suit me, as a husband, better than you.
In all your talk of marriage, you depict
A state that's gloomy, burdensome, and strict;
But, ah! when *he* describes the married state,
It sounds so sweet that I can hardly wait.

ARNOLPHE

Ah! So you love him, faithless girl!

AGNÈS

                              Why, yes.

ARNOLPHE

Have you the gall to tell me that, Agnès?

AGNÈS

If it's the truth, what's wrong with telling it?

ARNOLPHE

How dared you fall in love with him, you chit?

[*Act Five · Scene Four*]

AGNÈS

It was no fault of mine; he made me do it.
I was in love with him before I knew it.

ARNOLPHE

You should have overcome your amorous feeling.

AGNÈS

It's hard to overcome what's so appealing.

ARNOLPHE

Didn't you know that I would be put out?

AGNÈS

Why, no. What have you to complain about?

ARNOLPHE

Nothing, of course! I'm wild with happiness!
You don't, I take it, love me.

AGNÈS

Love you?

ARNOLPHE

Yes.

[*Act Five · Scene Four*]

AGNÈS

Alas, I don't.

ARNOLPHE

You *don't?*

AGNÈS

Would you have me lie?

ARNOLPHE

Why don't you love me, hussy? Tell me why!

AGNÈS

Good heavens, it's not I whom you should blame.
He made me love him; why didn't you do the same?
I didn't hinder you, as I recall.

ARNOLPHE

I tried to make you love me; I gave my all;
Yet all my pains and strivings were in vain.

AGNÈS

He has more aptitude than you, that's plain;
To win my heart, he scarcely had to try.

[*Act Five · Scene Four*]

ARNOLPHE, *aside*

This peasant girl can frame a neat reply!
What lady wit could answer with more art?
Either she's bright, or in what concerns the heart
A foolish girl can best the wisest man.
    (*To Agnès:*)
Well, then, Miss Back-Talk, answer this if you can:
Did I raise you, all these years, at such expense,
For another's benefit? Does that make sense?

AGNÈS

No. But he'll gladly pay you for your trouble.

ARNOLPHE, *aside*

Such flippancy! It makes my rage redouble.
    (*To Agnès:*)
You minx! How could he possibly discharge
Your obligations to me? They're too large.

AGNÈS

Frankly, they don't seem very large to me.

ARNOLPHE

Did I not nurture you from infancy?

AGNÈS

Yes, that you did. I'm deeply obligated.
How wondrously you've had me educated!

Do you fancy that I'm blind to what you've done,
And cannot see that I'm a simpleton?
Oh, it humiliates me; I revolt
Against the shame of being such a dolt.

ARNOLPHE

Do you think you'll gain the knowledge that you need
Through that young dandy's tutelage?

AGNÈS

                     Yes, indeed.
It's thanks to him I know what little I do;
I owe far more to him than I do to you.

ARNOLPHE

What holds me back, I ask myself, from treating
So insolent a girl to a sound beating?
Your coldness irks me to the point of tears,
And it would ease my soul to box your ears.

AGNÈS

Alas, then, beat me, if you so desire.

ARNOLPHE, *aside*

Those words and that sweet look dissolve my ire,
Restoring to my heart such tender feeling
As makes me quite forget her double-dealing.
How strange love is! How strange that men, from such
Perfidious beings, will endure so much!

130

[*Act Five · Scene Four*]

Women, as all men know, are frailly wrought:
They're foolish and illogical in thought,
Their souls are weak, their characters are bad,
There's nothing quite so silly, quite so mad,
So faithless; yet, despite these sorry features,
What won't we do to please the wretched creatures?
    (*To Agnès:*)
Come, traitress, let us be at peace once more.
I'll pardon you, and love you as before.
Repay my magnanimity, and learn
From my great love to love me in return.

AGNÈS

Truly, if I were able to, I would.
I'd gladly love you if I only could.

ARNOLPHE

You can, my little beauty, if you'll but try.
    (*He sighs.*)
Just listen to that deep and yearning sigh!
Look at my haggard face! See how it suffers!
Reject that puppy, and the love he offers:
He must have cast a spell on you; with me,
You'll be far happier, I guarantee.
I know that clothes and jewels are your passion;
Don't worry: you shall always be in fashion.
I'll pet you night and day; you shall be showered
With kisses; you'll be hugged, caressed, devoured.
And you shall have your wish in every way.
I'll say no more; what further could I say?
    (*Aside:*)
Lord, what extremes desire will drive us to!

131

[*Act Five · Scene Four*]

(*To Agnès:*)
In short, no love could match my love for you.
Tell me, ungrateful girl, what proof do you need?
Shall I weep? Or beat myself until I bleed?
What if I tore my hair out—would that sway you?
Shall I kill myself? Command, and I'll obey you.
I'm ready, cruel one, for you to prove me.

AGNÈS

Somehow, your lengthy speeches fail to move me.
Horace, in two words, could be more engaging.

ARNOLPHE

Enough of this! Your impudence is enraging.
I have my plans for you, you stubborn dunce,
And I shall pack you out of town at once.
You've spurned my love, and baited me as well—
Which you'll repent of in a convent cell.

132

SCENE FIVE

ALAIN, ARNOLPHE, AGNÈS

ALAIN

It's very strange, but Agnès has vanished, Sir.
I think that corpse has run away with her.

ARNOLPHE

She's here. Go shut her in my room, securely.
That's not where he'd come looking for her, surely,
And she'll be there but half an hour, at most.
Meanwhile I'll get a carriage, in which we'll post
To a safe retreat. Go now, and lock up tight,
And see that you don't let her out of sight.
          (*Alone:*)
Perhaps a change of scene and circumstance
Will wean her from this infantile romance.

SCENE SIX

HORACE, ARNOLPHE

HORACE

Seigneur Arnolphe, I'm overwhelmed with grief,
And Heaven's cruelty is beyond belief;
It seems now that a brutal stroke of fate
May force my love and me to separate.
My father, just this minute, chanced to appear,
Alighting from his coach not far from here,
And what has brought him into town this morning
Is a dire errand of which I'd had no warning:
He's made a match for me, and, ready or not,
I am to marry someone on the spot.
Imagine my despair! What blacker curse
Could fall on me, what setback could be worse?
I told you, yesterday, of Enrique. It's he
Who's brought about my present misery;
He's come with Father, to lead me to the slaughter,
And I am doomed to wed his only daughter.
When they told me that, it almost made me swoon;
And, since my father spoke of coming soon
To see you, I excused myself, in fright,
And hastened to forewarn you of my plight.
Take care, Sir, I entreat you, not to let him
Know of Agnès and me; 't would much upset him.
And try, since he so trusts your judgment, to
Dissuade him from the match he has in view.

134

[*Act Five · Scene Six*]

ARNOLPHE

I shall.

HORACE

That failing, you could be of aid
By urging that the wedding be delayed.

ARNOLPHE

Trust me.

HORACE

On you, my dearest hopes repose.

ARNOLPHE

Fine, fine.

HORACE

You're a father to me, Heaven knows.
Tell him that young men— Ah! He's coming! I spy him.
Here are some arguments with which to ply him.
(*They withdraw to a corner of the stage, and
confer in whispers.*)

SCENE SEVEN

ENRIQUE, ORONTE, CHRYSALDE, HORACE, ARNOLPHE

ENRIQUE, *to Chrysalde*

No need for introductions, Sir. I knew
Your name as soon as I set eyes on you.
You have the very features of your late
Sister, who was my well-belovèd mate;
Oh, how I wish that cruel Destiny
Had let me bring my helpmeet back with me,
After such years of hardship as we bore,
To see her home and family once more.
But fate has ruled that we shall not again
Enjoy her charming presence; let us, then,
Find solace in what joys we may design
For the sole offspring of her love and mine.
You are concerned in this; let us confer,
And see if you approve my plans for her.
Oronte's young son, I think, is a splendid choice;
But in this matter you've an equal voice.

CHRYSALDE

I've better judgment, Brother, than to question
So eminently worthy a suggestion.

ARNOLPHE, *to Horace*

Yes, yes, don't worry; I'll represent you well.

HORACE

Once more, don't tell him—

ARNOLPHE

I promise not to tell.
(*Arnolphe leaves Horace, and crosses to
embrace Oronte.*)

ORONTE

Ah, my old friend: what a warm, hearty greeting!

ARNOLPHE

Oronte, dear fellow, what a welcome meeting!

ORONTE

I've come to town—

ARNOLPHE

You needn't say a word;
I know what brings you.

ORONTE

You've already heard?

ARNOLPHE

Yes.

ORONTE

Good.

ARNOLPHE

      Your son regards this match with dread;
His heart rebels at being forced to wed,
And I've been asked, in fact, to plead his case.
Well, do you know what I'd do, in your place?
I'd exercise a father's rightful sway
And tie the wedding knot without delay.
What the young need, my friend, is discipline;
We only do them harm by giving in.

HORACE, *aside*

Traitor!

CHRYSALDE

      If the prospect fills him with revulsion,
Then surely we should not employ compulsion.
My brother-in-law, I trust, would say the same.

ARNOLPHE

Shall a man be governed by his son? For shame!
Would you have a father be so meek and mild
As not to exact obedience from his child?

At his wise age, 't would be grotesque indeed
To see him led by one whom he should lead.
No, no; my dear old friend is honor-bound;
He's given his word, and he must not give ground.
Let him be firm, as a father should, and force
His son to take the necessary course.

ORONTE

Well said: we shall proceed with this alliance,
And I shall answer for my son's compliance.

CHRYSALDE, *to Arnolphe*

It much surprises me to hear you press
For this betrothal with such eagerness.
What is your motive? I can't make you out.

ARNOLPHE

Don't worry, friend; I know what I'm about.

ORONTE

Indeed, Arnolphe—

CHRYSALDE

He finds that name unpleasant.
Monsieur de la Souche is what he's called at present.

ARNOLPHE

No matter.

[*Act Five · Scene Seven*]

HORACE

What do I hear?

ARNOLPHE, *turning toward Horace*

               Well, now you know,
And now you see why I have spoken so.

HORACE

Oh, what confusion—

SCENE EIGHT

GEORGETTE, ENRIQUE, ORONTE, CHRYSALDE,
HORACE, ARNOLPHE

GEORGETTE

Sir, please come. Unless
You do, I fear we can't restrain Agnès.
The girl is frantic to escape, I swear,
And might jump out of the window in despair.

ARNOLPHE

Bring her to me: I'll take her away from here
Posthaste, this very minute.
(*To Horace:*)
Be of good cheer.
Too much good luck could spoil you; and, as they say
In the proverb, every dog must have his day.

HORACE

What man, O Heaven, was ever betrayed like this,
Or hurled into so hopeless an abyss?

ARNOLPHE, *to Oronte*

Pray don't delay the nuptials—which, dear friend,
I shall be most delighted to attend.

ORONTE

I shan't delay.

141

SCENE NINE

ARNOLPHE

Come, come, my pretty child,
You who are so intractable and wild.
Here is your gallant: perhaps he should receive
A little curtsey from you, as you leave.
(*To Horace:*)
Farewell: your sweet hopes seem to have turned to gall;
But love, my boy, can't always conquer all.

AGNÈS

Horace! Will you let him take me away from you?

HORACE

I'm dazed with grief, and don't know what to do.

ARNOLPHE

Come, chatterbox.

AGNÈS

No. Here I shall remain.

[*Act Five · Scene Nine*]

ORONTE

Now, what's the mystery? Will you please explain?
All this is very odd; we're baffled by it.

ARNOLPHE

When I've more time, I'll gladly clarify it.
Till then, good-bye.

ORONTE

          Where is it you mean to go?
And why won't you tell us what we ask to know?

ARNOLPHE

I've told you that, despite your stubborn son,
You ought to hold the wedding.

ORONTE

              It shall be done.
But weren't you told that his intended spouse
Is the young woman who's living in your house—
The long-lost child of that dear Angélique
Who secretly was married to Enrique?
What, then, did your behavior mean just now?

CHRYSALDE

His words amazed me, too, I must allow.

[*Act Five · Scene Nine*]

ARNOLPHE

What? What?

CHRYSALDE

My sister married secretly;
Her daughter's birth was kept from the family.

ORONTE

The child was placed with an old country dame,
Who reared her under a fictitious name.

CHRYSALDE

My sister's husband, beset by circumstance,
Was soon obliged to take his leave of France,

ORONTE

And undergo great trials and miseries
In a strange, savage land beyond the seas,

CHRYSALDE

Where, through his labors, he regained abroad
What here he'd lost through men's deceit and fraud.

ORONTE

Returning home, he sought at once to find
The nurse to whom his child had been consigned,

144

CHRYSALDE

And the good creature told him, as was true,
That she'd transferred her little charge to you,

ORONTE

Because of your benevolent disposition,
And the dire poverty of her condition.

CHRYSALDE

What's more, Enrique, transported with delight,
Has brought the woman here to set things right.

ORONTE

She'll join us in a moment, and then we'll see
A public end to all this mystery.

CHRYSALDE, *to Arnolphe*

I know that you're in a painful state of mind;
Yet what the Fates have done is not unkind.
Since your chief treasure is a hornless head,
The safest course, for you, is not to wed.

ARNOLPHE, *leaving in a speechless passion*

Oof!

ORONTE

Why is he rushing off without a word?

HORACE

Father, a great coincidence has occurred.
What in your wisdom you projected, chance
Has wondrously accomplished in advance.
The fact is, Sir, that I am bound already,
By the sweet ties of love, to this fair lady;
It's she whom you have come to seek, and she
For whose sake I opposed your plans for me.

ENRIQUE

I recognized her from the very first,
With such deep joy, I thought my heart would burst.
Dear daughter, let me take you in my embrace.
                    (*He does so.*)

CHRYSALDE

I have the same urge, Brother, but this place
Will hardly do for private joys like these.
Let us go in, resolve all mysteries,
Commend our friend Arnolphe, and for the rest
Thank Heaven, which orders all things for the best.